Simply the Best of
TINA TURNER

ISBN 1-57560-749-2

Cherry Lane Music Company
Director of Publications/Project Editor: Mark Phillips

Copyright © 2004 Cherry Lane Music Company
International Copyright Secured   All Rights Reserved

The music, text, design and graphics in this publication are protected by copyright law. Any duplication or transmission, by any means, electronic, mechanical, photocopying, recording or otherwise, is an infringement of copyright.

Visit our website at www.cherrylane.com

CONTENTS

- 4   The Best
- 11   I Can't Stand the Rain
- 14   Better Be Good to Me
- 18   I Don't Wanna Fight
- 23   Private Dancer
- 28   Let's Stay Together
- 38   Nutbush City Limits
- 40   Proud Mary
- 47   River Deep - Mountain High
- 54   Typical Male
- 60   What's Love Got to Do with It
- 66   We Don't Need Another Hero

TINA TURNER

Tina Turner's solo career famously ignited 15 years ago, but we all know the epic tale that had already spun out before *Private Dancer* came to be. When you look at the dates, you might think your calculator is on the blink. That voracious passion for baring her soul in the studio and onstage has now been on public record for more than 45 years. In her seminal soul tome *Nowhere to Run*, writer Gerri Hirshey talks of the vocal performance at a 1953 session by a barely teenage Tina as sounding like "a starving child singing for its supper," and the better part of half a century later she still has that same appetite.

Born in Brownsville, Tennessee, and raised nearby in the "li'l ol' town" of Nutbush, just like the song says, Anna Mae Bullock and her older sister Alline relocated to St. Louis in 1956. She knew rejection only too well even then, the sisters having been deserted by their mother and later their father. And when Annie first asked the leader of local club favorites the Kings of Rhythm if she could sing with them, the answer from Ike Turner was another firm no.

Persistence, as we know, paid off. Ike and Tina, as she now was, were married in 1958 and Tina began regular work as the band's singer. Their first historic single together happened by one of those fateful chances that the record industry seems to specialize in. In the autumn of 1960, the session singer booked to record Ike's "A Fool in Love" didn't show. Tina stepped in; an R&B smash and U.S. Top 30 pop crossover ensued, and soon the band was going by a new name: The Ike & Tina Turner Revue.

The duo's track record in the '60s and early '70s, both on cast-iron anthems like "River Deep - Mountain High" and "Nutbush City Limits" and lesser-feted soul classics like "I Can't Believe What You Say," is the stuff of legend, as, sadly, is the violent disintegration of the Turners' marriage. But, emboldened by her newly found Buddhist faith and big-screen solo success as the Acid Queen in the Who's *Tommy*, Tina struck out on her own in the summer of 1976.

At first, she stood at the bottom of what seemed an impossible mountain of debts and disinterest from the industry. While other soul divas made good in a world that she had inspired them to enter, Tina was living for a time on food stamps. Her name still got her onto TV game shows and then the supper club circuit in Las Vegas. Then, in 1979, Tina met Roger Davies, a young Australian manager who'd recently relocated to Los Angeles and took the challenge of redefining one of the great lost vocalists and performers of the age.

With Davies' help, Turner refound the rock 'n' roll raunch of her best records, infused it with her intuitive soulfulness, and started again. A 1981 support slot on the Rolling Stones' U.S. tour led to an invitation from Heaven 17's Ian Craig Marsh and Martyn Ware for Tina to take part on their multi-artist *Music of Quality and Distinction, Volume 1* album. Before the end of 1982, she had a new solo deal with Capitol Records.

By the summer of 1984, fuelled by the acclaim that met the leadoff single, "What's Love Got to Do with It," *Private Dancer* was on its way to world sales of 11 million.

What's followed has been an extraordinary catalogue of collaborations and achievements on record, on the big screen, and as an author: a role as Aunty Entity alongside Mel Gibson in *Mad Max: Beyond Thunderdome*; a duet with Mick Jagger at the greatest live event in music history, Live Aid; a raft of Grammy Awards; a bestselling autobiography, *I, Tina*, leading to the hit biopic *What's Love Got to Do with It*; record and concert dates with avowed Turner fans like Bryan Adams, Rod Stewart, Elton John, David Bowie, Eric Clapton, and Mark Knopfler; and record-breaking concert tours, including sellout shows in such singular locations as the Maracana Stadium in Rio and England's Woburn Abbey. Her U2-penned smash hit from the Bond movie *GoldenEye* and her stadium tour of Europe in 1996 saw her smash box office records in ten countries playing to over three million people.

The Best

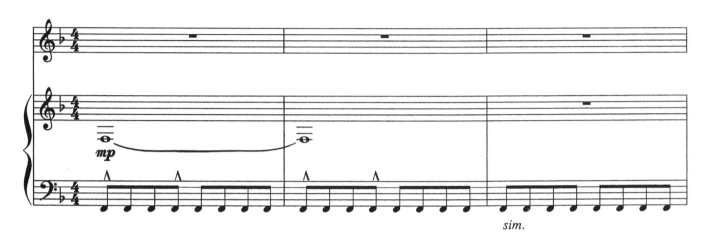

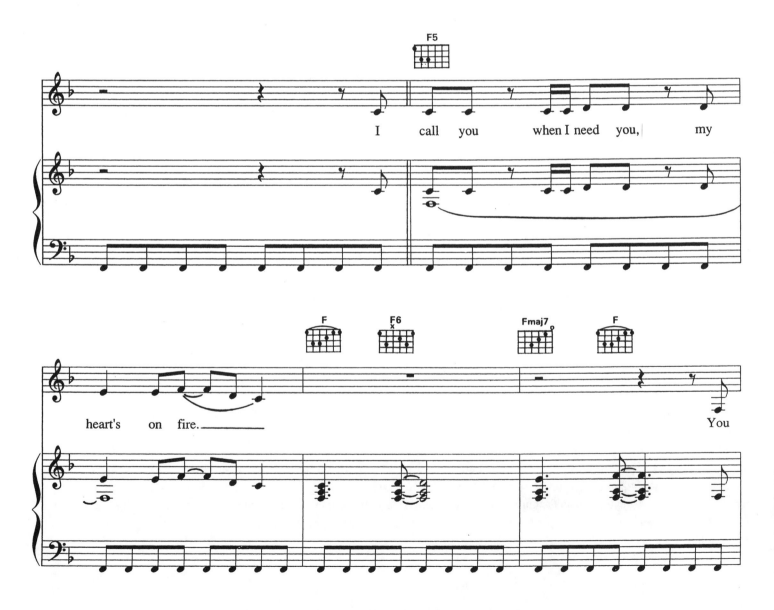

© 1989 KNIGHTY-KNIGHT MUSIC and MIKE CHAPMAN PUBLISHING ENTERPRISES
All Rights for MIKE CHAPMAN PUBLISHING ENTERPRISES Controlled and Administered by MUSIC & MEDIA INTERNATIONAL, INC.
All Rights Reserved International Copyright Secured Used by Permission

Additional Lyrics

Verse 2: In your heart at the start of every night and every day,
In your eyes I get lost, I get washed away.
Just as long as I'm here in your arms
I could be in no better place.

You're simply the best. . . . . .

I Can't Stand the Rain

Words and Music by
Don Bryant, Ann Peebles
and Bernard Miller

Better Be Good to Me

Words and Music by
Mike Chapman, Nicky Chinn
and Holly Knight

14

Private Dancer

Words and Music by
Mark Knopfler

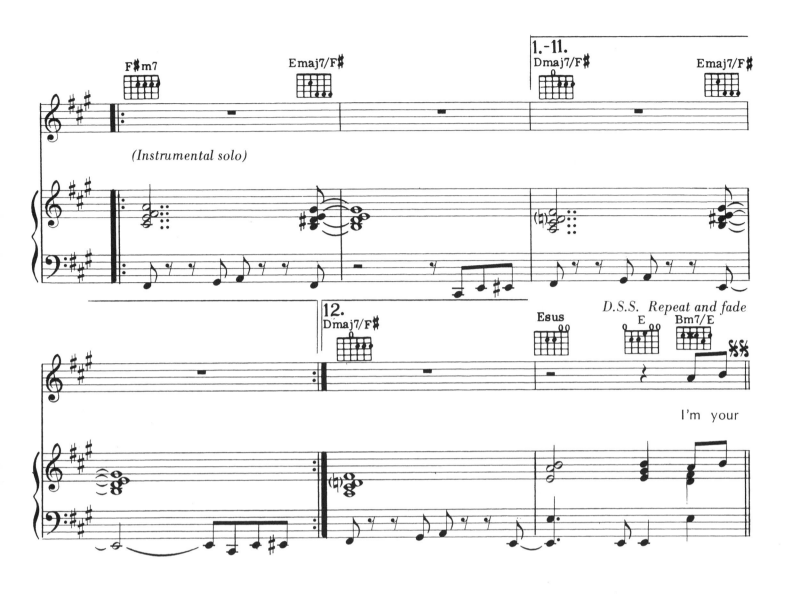

Verse 2:
You don't think of them as human.
You don't think of them at all.
You keep your mind on the money,
Keeping your eyes on the wall.

(To Chorus:)

Verse 3:
I want to make a million dollars.
I want to live out by the sea.
Have a husband and some children;
Yeah, I guess I want a family.

Let's Stay Together

Words and Music by
Al Green, Willie Mitchell
and Al Jackson, Jr.

* Recorded a half step lower.

Copyright © 1971, 1972 IRVING MUSIC, INC., AL GREEN MUSIC, INC. and AL JACKSON, JR. MUSIC (BMI)/ Administered by BUG MUSIC
Copyright Renewed
All Rights for AL GREEN MUSIC, INC. Administered by IRVING MUSIC, INC.
All Rights Reserved   Used by Permission

Nutbush City Limits

Words and Music by
Tina Turner

© 1973 (Renewed 2001) EMI BLACKWOOD MUSIC INC. and EMI UNART CATALOG INC.
All Rights Administered by EMI UNART CATALOG INC. (Publishing) and WARNER BROS. PUBLICATIONS U.S. INC. (Print)
All Rights Reserved   Used by Permission

Proud Mary

Words and Music by
J.C. Fogerty

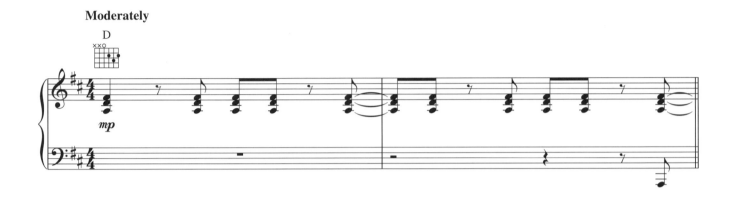

Recitation:
You know, every now and then I think you might like to hear something from us nice an' easy.
But there's just one thing. You see, we never ever do nothin' nice an' easy.
We always do it nice an' rough.
Now, we're gonna take the beginning of this song and do it easy.
But then we're gonna do the finish rough.
That's the way we do "Proud Mary."

© 1968 (Renewed) JONDORA MUSIC
All Rights Reserved   Used by Permission

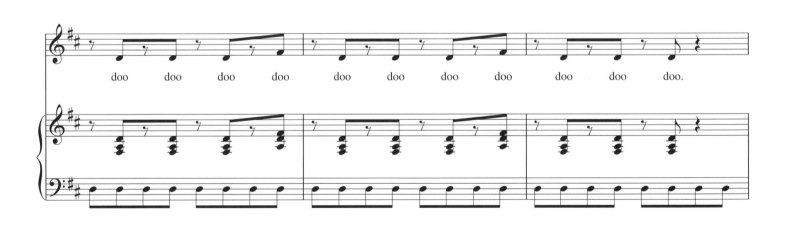
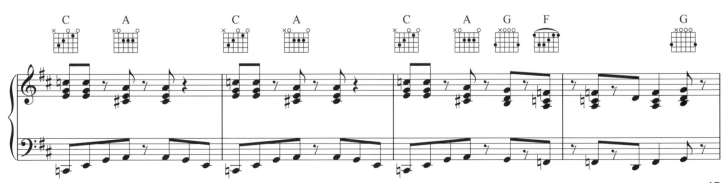

River Deep - Mountain High

Words and Music by
Jeff Barry, Ellie Greenwich
and Phil Spector

© 1966, 1967 (Renewed) TRIO MUSIC COMPANY, INC., MOTHER BERTHA MUSIC, INC.
and UNIVERSAL - POLYGRAM INTERNATIONAL PUBLISHING, INC.
All Rights on behalf of MOTHER BERTHA MUSIC, INC. administered by ABKCO MUSIC, INC.
All Rights Reserved

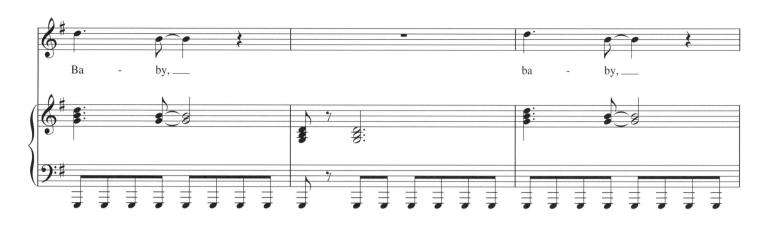
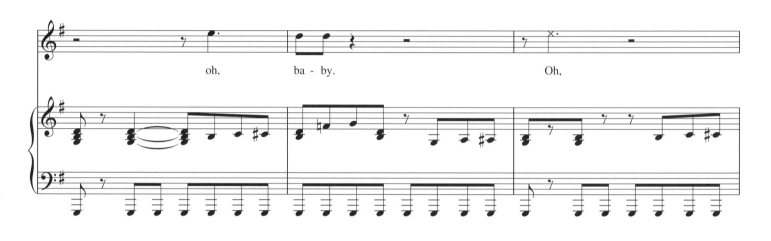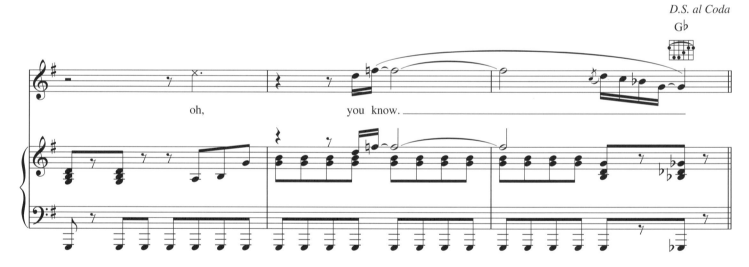

Typical Male

Words and Music by
Terry Britten and Graham Lyle

Medium Funk

Tell me law-yer what to do, I think I'm fall-ing in love with you. Mm, mm, de-fend me from the way I feel.

male. Your sense of jus-tice I'll em-brace, but your de-fense don't help my case. Mm, mm, I'm deep in trou-ble with the law.

© 1986 MYAXE MUSIC, LTD. and GOOD SINGLE LIMITED
All Rights for MYAXE MUSIC, LTD. Administered by WB MUSIC CORP.
All Rights for GOOD SINGLE LIMITED Administered by SONGS OF WINDSWEPT PACIFIC
All Rights Reserved Used by Permission

What's Love Got to Do with It

Verse 2:
It may seem to you
That I'm acting confused
When you're close to me.
If I tend to look dazed,
I read it some place;
I've got cause to be.
There's a name for it,
There's a phrase that fits,
But whatever the reason,
You do it for me.

(To Chorus)

We Don't Need Another Hero

Words and Music by
Terry Britten and Graham Lyle

Verse 3:
Looking for something we can rely on;
There's got to be something better out there.

Verse 4:
Love and compassion; that day is coming.
All else are castles built in the air.

(To Bridge I)

More Great Piano/Vocal Books
FROM CHERRY LANE

For a complete listing of Cherry Lane titles available, including contents listings, please visit our web site at
www.cherrylane.com

02500343 Almost Famous. $14.95	02500693 Dave Matthews – Some Devil . . $16.95	02500344 Billy Strayhorn:
02502171 The Best of Boston $17.95	02500555 Dave Matthews Band –	An American Master $17.95
02500672 Black Eyed Peas – Elephunk. . . $17.95	Busted Stuff $16.95	02502132 Barbra Streisand –
02500665 Sammy Cahn Songbook $24.95	02500003 Dave Matthews Band –	Back to Broadway. $19.95
02500144 Mary Chapin Carpenter –	These Crowded Streets $17.95	02500515 Barbra Streisand –
Party Doll & Other Favorites . . $16.95	02502199 Dave Matthews Band – Crash . . $17.95	Christmas Memories. $16.95
02502163 Mary Chapin Carpenter –	02500390 Dave Matthews Band –	02507969 Barbra Streisand – A Collection:
Stones in the Road $17.95	Everyday $14.95	Greatest Hits and More $17.95
02502165 John Denver Anthology –	02500493 Dave Matthews Band – Live in Chicago	02502164 Barbra Streisand – The Concert $22.95
Revised. $22.95	12/19/98 at the United Center $14.95	02500550 Essential Barbra Streisand $24.95
02502227 John Denver –	02502192 Dave Matthews Band – Under	02502228 Barbra Streisand –
A Celebration of Life $14.95	the Table and Dreaming $17.95	Higher Ground $16.95
02500002 John Denver Christmas. $14.95	02500681 John Mayer – Heavier Things . . $16.95	02500196 Barbra Streisand –
02502166 John Denver's Greatest Hits. . . . $17.95	02500563 John Mayer – Room for Squares $16.95	A Love Like Ours. $16.95
02502151 John Denver – A Legacy	02500081 Natalie Merchant – Ophelia . . . $14.95	02500280 Barbra Streisand – Timeless . . . $19.95
in Song (Softcover). $24.95	02500423 Natalie Merchant – Tigerlily . . . $14.95	02503617 John Tesh – Avalon. $15.95
02502152 John Denver – A Legacy	02502895 Nine $17.95	02502178 The John Tesh Collection $17.95
in Song (Hardcover). $34.95	02500425 Time and Love: The Art and	02503623 John Tesh – A Family Christmas $15.95
02500566 Poems, Prayers and Promises: The Art	Soul of Laura Nyro $19.95	02505511 John Tesh –
and Soul of John Denver $19.95	02502204 The Best of Metallica $17.95	Favorites for Easy Piano $12.95
02500326 John Denver –	02500407 O-Town $14.95	02503630 John Tesh – Grand Passion. . . . $16.95
The Wildlife Concert $17.95	02500010 Tom Paxton – The Honor	02500124 John Tesh – One World $14.95
02500501 John Denver and the Muppets:	of Your Company $17.95	02500307 John Tesh – Pure Movies 2 . . . . $16.95
A Christmas Together $9.95	02507962 Peter, Paul & Mary –	02500565 Thoroughly Modern Millie $17.95
02509922 The Songs of Bob Dylan $29.95	Holiday Concert $17.95	02500576 Toto – 5 of the Best $7.95
02500586 Linda Eder – Broadway My Way $14.95	02500145 Pokemon 2.B.A. Master $12.95	02502175 Tower of Power –
02500497 Linda Eder – Gold $14.95	02500026 The Prince of Egypt $16.95	Silver Anniversary $17.95
02500396 Linda Eder –	02500660 Best of Bonnie Raitt $17.95	02502198 The "Weird Al" Yankovic
Christmas Stays the Same. . . . $17.95	02502189 The Bonnie Raitt Collection. . . . $22.95	Anthology. $17.95
02500175 Linda Eder –	02502230 Bonnie Raitt – Fundamental . . . $17.95	02502217 Trisha Yearwood –
It's No Secret Anymore $14.95	02502139 Bonnie Raitt –	A Collection of Hits $16.95
02502209 Linda Eder – It's Time $17.95	Longing in Their Hearts. $16.95	02500334 Maury Yeston – December Songs $17.95
02500630 Donald Fagen – 5 of the Best . . . $7.95	02502088 Bonnie Raitt – Luck of the Draw $14.95	02502225 The Maury Yeston Songbook. . . $19.95
02500535 Erroll Garner Anthology $19.95	02507958 Bonnie Raitt – Nick of Time . . . $14.95	
02500270 Gilbert & Sullivan for Easy Piano $12.95	02502190 Bonnie Raitt – Road Tested. . . . $24.95	See your local music dealer or contact:
02500318 Gladiator $12.95	02502218 Kenny Rogers – The Gift $16.95	
02500273 Gold & Glory:	02500072 Saving Private Ryan. $14.95	
The Road to El Dorado $16.95	02500197 SHeDAISY –	
02502126 Best of Guns N' Roses. $17.95	The Whole SHeBANG. $14.95	
02502072 Guns N' Roses – Selections from	02500414 Shrek. $14.95	
Use Your Illusion I and II $17.95	02500536 Spirit – Stallion of the Cimarron $16.95	
02500014 Sir Roland Hanna Collection . . . $19.95	02500166 Steely Dan – Anthology. $17.95	
02500352 Hanson – This Time Around . . . $16.95	02500622 Steely Dan –	
02502134 Best of Lenny Kravitz. $12.95	Everything Must Go $14.95	
02500012 Lenny Kravitz – 5 . . . . $16.95	02500284 Steely Dan –	
02500381 Lenny Kravitz – Greatest Hits. . . $14.95	Two Against Nature $14.95	
02503701 Man of La Mancha $10.95	02500165 Best of Steely Dan. $14.95	

CHERRY LANE MUSIC COMPANY
6 East 32nd Street, New York, NY 10016
Quality in Printed Music

EXCLUSIVELY DISTRIBUTED BY

7777 W. BLUEMOUND RD. P.O. BOX 13819 MILWAUKEE, WI 53213

Prices, contents and availability subject to change without notice.
0404

More Big-Note & Easy Piano Books

For a complete listing of Cherry Lane titles available, including contents listings, please visit our web site at www.cherrylane.com

CLASSICAL CHRISTMAS
Easy solo arrangements of 30 wonderful holiday songs: Ave Maria • Dance of the Sugar Plum Fairy • Evening Prayer • Gesu Bambino • Hallelujah! He Shall Feed His Flock • March of the Toys • O Come, All Ye Faithful • O Holy Night • Pastoral Symphony • Sheep May Safely Graze • Sinfonia • Waltz of the Flowers • and more.
__02500112 Easy Piano Solo $9.95

BEST OF JOHN DENVER
__02505512 Easy Piano $9.95

DOWN THE AISLE
Easy piano arrangements of 20 beloved pop and classical wedding songs, including: Air on the G String • Ave Maria • Canon in D • Follow Me • Give Me Forever (I Do) • Jesu, Joy of Man's Desiring • Prince of Denmark's March • Through the Years • Trumpet Tune • Unchained Melody • Wedding March • When I Fall in Love • You Decorated My Life • and more.
__025000267 Easy Piano $9.95

EASY BROADWAY SHOWSTOPPERS
Easy piano arrangements of 16 traditional and new Broadway standards, including: "Impossible Dream" from *Man of La Mancha* • "Unusual Way" from *Nine* • "This Is the Moment" from *Jekyll & Hyde* • many more.
__02505517 Easy Piano $12.95

GOLD AND GLORY – THE ROAD TO EL DORADO
This beautiful souvenir songbook features full-color photos and 8 songs from the DreamWorks animated film. Includes original songs by Elton John and Tim Rice, and a score by Hans Zimmer and John Powell. Songs: Cheldorado – Score • El Dorado • Friends Never Say Goodbye • It's Tough to Be a God • Someday out of the Blue (Theme from El Dorado) • The Trail We Blaze • Without Question • Wonders of the New World: To Shibalba.
__02500274 Easy Piano $14.95

A FAMILY CHRISTMAS AROUND THE PIANO
25 songs for hours of family fun, including: Away in a Manger • Deck the Hall • The First Noel • God Rest Ye Merry, Gentlemen • Hark! the Herald Angels Sing • Jingle Bells • Jolly Old St. Nicholas • Joy to the World • O Little Town of Bethlehem • Silent Night, Holy Night • The Twelve Days of Christmas • and more.
__02500398 Easy Piano $7.95

GILBERT & SULLIVAN FOR EASY PIANO
20 great songs from 6 great shows by this beloved duo renowned for their comedic classics. Includes: Behold the Lord High Executioner • The Flowers That Bloom in the Spring • He Is an Englishman • I Am the Captain of the Pinafore • (I'm Called) Little Buttercup • Miya Sama • Three Little Maids • Tit-Willow • We Sail the Ocean Blue • When a Merry Maiden Marries • When Britain Really Ruled the Waves • When Frederic Was a Lad • and more.
__02500270 Easy Piano $12.95

GREAT CONTEMPORARY BALLADS
__02500150 Easy Piano $12.95

HOLY CHRISTMAS CAROLS COLORING BOOK
A terrific songbook with 7 sacred carols and lots of coloring pages for the young pianist. Songs include: Angels We Have Heard on High • The First Noel • Hark! The Herald Angels Sing • It Came upon a Midnight Clear • O Come All Ye Faithful • O Little Town of Bethlehem • Silent Night.
__02500277 Five-Finger Piano $6.95

JEKYLL & HYDE – VOCAL SELECTIONS
Ten songs from the Wildhorn/Bricusse Broadway smash, arranged for big-note: In His Eyes • It's a Dangerous Game • Lost in the Darkness • A New Life • No One Knows Who I Am • Once Upon a Dream • Someone Like You • Sympathy, Tenderness • Take Me as I Am • This Is the Moment.
__02505515 Easy Piano $12.95
__02500023 Big-Note Piano $9.95

JUST FOR KIDS – *NOT!* CHRISTMAS SONGS
This unique collection of 14 Christmas favorites is fun for the whole family! Kids can play the full-sounding big-note solos alone, or with their parents (or teachers) playing accompaniment for the thrill of four-hand piano! Includes: Deck the Halls • Jingle Bells • Silent Night • What Child Is This? • and more.
__02505510 Big-Note Piano $7.95

JUST FOR KIDS – *NOT!* CLASSICS
Features big-note arrangements of classical masterpieces, plus optional accompaniment for adults. Songs: Air on the G String • Dance of the Sugar Plum Fairy • Für Elise • Jesu, Joy of Man's Desiring • Ode to Joy • Pomp and Circumstance • The Sorcerer's Apprentice • William Tell Overture • and more!
__02505513 Classics...................$7.95
__02500301 More Classics $7.95

JUST FOR KIDS – *NOT!* FUN SONGS
Fun favorites for kids everywhere in big-note arrangements for piano, including: Bingo • Eensy Weensy Spider • Farmer in the Dell • Jingle Bells • London Bridge • Pop Goes the Weasel • Puff the Magic Dragon • Skip to My Lou • Twinkle, Twinkle Little Star • and more!
__02505523 Fun Songs................$7.95
__02505528 More Fun Songs $7.95

JUST FOR KIDS – *NOT!* TV THEMES & MOVIE SONGS
Entice the kids to the piano with this delightful collection of songs and themes from movies and TV. These big-note arrangements include themes from The Brady Bunch and The Addams Family, as well as Do-Re-Mi (The Sound of Music), theme from Beetlejuice (Day-O) and Puff the Magic Dragon. Each song includes an accompaniment part for teacher or adult so that the kids can experience the joy of four-hand playing as well! Plus performance tips.
__02505507 TV Themes & Movie Songs $9.95
__02500304 More TV Themes & Movie Songs $9.95

LOVE BALLADS
__02500152 EZ-Play Today #364 $7.95

MERRY CHRISTMAS, EVERYONE
Over 20 contemporary and classic all-time holiday favorites arranged for big-note piano or easy piano. Includes: Away in a Manger • Christmas Like a Lullaby • The First Noel • Joy to the World • The Marvelous Toy • and more.
__02505600 Big-Note Piano $9.95

See your local music dealer or contact:

CHERRY LANE MUSIC COMPANY
6 East 32nd Street, New York, NY 10016

EXCLUSIVELY DISTRIBUTED BY

7777 W. BLUEMOUND RD. P.O. BOX 13819 MILWAUKEE, WI 53213

POKEMON 2 B.A. MASTER
This great songbook features easy piano arrangements of 13 tunes from the hit TV series: 2.B.A. Master • Double Trouble (Team Rocket) • Everything Changes • Misty's Song • My Best Friends • Pokémon (Dance Mix) • Pokémon Theme • PokéRAP • The Time Has Come (Pikachu's Goodbye) • Together, Forever • Viridian City • What Kind of Pokémon Are You? • You Can Do It (If You Really Try). Includes a full-color, 8-page pull-out section featuring characters and scenes from this super hot show.
__02500145 Easy Piano $12.95

POKEMON
Five-finger arrangements of 7 songs from the hottest show for kids! Includes: Pokémon Theme • The Time Has Come (Pikachu's Goodbye) • 2B A Master • Together, Forever • What Kind of Pokémon Are You? • You Can Do It (If You Really Try). Also features cool character artwork, and a special section listing the complete lyrics for the "PokéRAP."
__02500291 Five-Finger Piano $7.95

POP/ROCK HITS
__02500153 E-Z Play Today #366 $7.95

POP/ROCK LOVE SONGS
Easy arrangements of 18 romatic favorites, including: Always • Bed of Roses • Butterfly Kisses • Follow Me • From This Moment On • Hard Habit to Break • Leaving on a Jet Plane • When You Say Nothing at All • more.
__02500151 Easy Piano $10.95

POPULAR CHRISTMAS CAROLS COLORING BOOK
Kids are sure to love this fun holiday songbook! It features five-finger piano arrangements of seven Christmas classics, complete with coloring pages throughout! Songs include: Deck the Hall • Good King Wenceslas • Jingle Bells • Jolly Old St. Nicholas • O Christmas Tree • Up on the Housetop • We Wish You a Merry Christmas.
__02500276 Five-Finger Piano $6.95

PUFF THE MAGIC DRAGON & 54 OTHER ALL-TIME CHILDREN'S FAVORITE SONGS
55 timeless songs enjoyed by generations of kids, and sure to be favorites for years to come. Songs include: A-Tisket A-Tasket • Alouette • Eensy Weensy Spider • The Farmer in the Dell • I've Been Working on the Railroad • If You're Happy and You Know It • Joy to the World • Michael Finnegan • Oh Where, Oh Where Has My Little Dog Gone • Silent Night • Skip to My Lou • This Old Man • and many more.
__02500017 Big-Note Piano $12.95

PURE ROMANCE
__02500268 Easy Piano $10.95

SCHOOLHOUSE ROCK SONGBOOK
10 unforgettable songs from the classic television educational series, now experiencing a booming resurgence in popularity from Generation X'ers to today's kids! Includes: I'm Just a Bill • Conjunction Junction • Lolly, Lolly, Lolly (Get Your Adverbs Here) • The Great American Melting Pot • and more.
__02505576 Big-Note Piano $8.95

BEST OF JOHN TESH
__02505511 Easy Piano $12.95
__02500128 E-Z Play Today #356 $8.95

TOP COUNTRY HITS
__02500154 E-Z Play Today #365 $7.95

Prices, contents, and availability subject to change without notice.

DreamWorks Pictures™

Cherry Lane Music is proud to be the exclusive print music publisher for DreamWorks Pictures™. We are pleased to present folios and sheet music for the following critically acclaimed movies:

Almost Famous – Highlights

12 songs from the Grammy Award-winning soundtrack to the poignant movie that Cameron Crowe calls his "love letter back to music." This souvenir folio includes an introduction, photos from the film, hits from the '70s, and some songs from the repertoire of Stillwater, the fictional band portrayed in the movie. Songs include: America (Simon & Garfunkel) • Every Picture Tells a Story (Rod Stewart) • Fever Dog (Stillwater) • Lucky Trumble (Nancy Wilson) • Mr. Farmer (The Seeds) • That's the Way (Led Zeppelin) • Tiny Dancer (Elton John) • The Wind (Cat Stevens) • and more.
_____02500343 P/V/G..........................$14.95

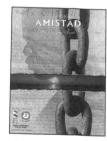

Amistad

Score composed by John Williams

Selections from the groundbreaking Steven Spielberg film include the resplendent main theme, "Dry Your Tears, Afrika." Also features photos from the film, as well as historical background and commentary from both Williams and Spielberg.
_____02501801 Piano/Vocal $14.95

Gold and Glory: The Road to El Dorado

This beautiful souvenir songbook features full-color photos and 8 songs from the DreamWorks animated film. Includes original songs by Elton John and Tim Rice, and a score by Hans Zimmer and John Powell. Songs: Cheldorado – Score • El Dorado • Friends Never Say Goodbye • It's Tough to Be a God • Someday out of the Blue (Theme from El Dorado) • The Trail We Blaze • Without Question • Wonders of the New World: To Shibalba.
_____02500274 Easy Piano $14.95
_____02500273 P/V/G..........................$16.95

Gladiator

Music from the Motion Picture

This terrific collection contains piano solo arrangements of 8 songs by Hans Zimmer and Lisa Gerrard from this summer's big blockbuster! Includes: Am I Not Merciful? • Barbarian Horde • The Battle • Earth • Honor Him • The Might of Rome • Now We Are Free • Slaves to Rome. Also includes a fantastic 8-page section featuring full-color photos from the film!
_____02500318 Piano Solo..................$12.95

Prince of Egypt

Original songs by Stephen Schwartz and Diane Warren
Score composed by Hans Zimmer

Selections from the acclaimed DreamWorks animated film include all feature songs by Stephen Schwartz ("All I Ever Wanted," "Deliver Us," "When You Believe" and more) as well as themes from the Hans Zimmer soundtrack. Fully illustrated throughout with color reproductions of the stunning artwork!
_____02500026 P/V/G..........................$16.95
_____02500027 Easy Piano $14.95
Also Available:
_____02500028 Recorder Fun! $9.95

Prices, contents, and availability subject to change without notice.

CHERRY LANE MUSIC COMPANY
6 East 32nd Street, New York, NY 10016

Quality in Printed Music

Saving Private Ryan

Score composed by John Williams

Selections from the heralded Steven Spielberg film include the moving "Hymn to the Fallen." Plus color photos, historical and background information on the making of the film from Steven Spielberg, Tom Hanks, and other cast members.
_____02500072 Piano Solo $14.95

Shrek

7 songs from the soundtrack of this innovative animated film. Includes: All Star • I'm a Believer • I'm on My Way • It Is You (I Have Loved) • Stay Home • True Love's First Kiss • You Belong to Me.
_____02500414 P/V/G..........................$14.95

SHEET MUSIC

For Always
(from *A.I.*)
_____02500449 Piano/Vocal $3.95

Hymn to the Fallen
(from *Saving Private Ryan*)
_____02500030 Piano/Vocal $3.95

Someday Out of the Blue
(Elton John)
(Theme from *The Road to El Dorado*)
_____02500289 Piano/Vocal $3.95

When You Believe
(Whitney Houston & Mariah Carey)
(from *Prince of Egypt*)
_____02500082 P/V/G $3.95
_____02500109 Easy Piano $3.95

EXCLUSIVELY DISTRIBUTED BY

7777 W. BLUEMOUND RD. P.O. BOX 13819 MILWAUKEE, WI 53213

Visit Cherry Lane on the Internet at **www.cherrylane.com**

great songs series

Cherry Lane Music is proud to present this legendary series which has delighted players and performers for generations.

Great Songs of the Fifties

The latest release in Cherry Lane's acclaimed Great Songs series, this songbook presents 51 musical memories from the fabulous '50s! Features rock, pop, country, Broadway and movie tunes, including: All Shook Up • At the Hop • Blue Suede Shoes • Dream Lover • Fly Me to the Moon • Kansas City • Love Me Tender • Misty • Peggy Sue • Rock Around the Clock • Sea of Love • Sixteen Tons • Take the "A" Train • Wonderful! Wonderful! • and more. Includes an introduction by award-winning journalist Bruce Pollock.
_____02500323 P/V/G..............$16.95

Great Songs of the Sixties, Vol. 1 – Revised Edition

The newly updated version of this classic book includes 80 faves from the 1960s: Angel of the Morning • Bridge over Troubled Water • Cabaret • Different Drum • Do You Believe in Magic • Eve of Destruction • Georgy Girl • It Was a Very Good Year • Monday, Monday • People • Spinning Wheel • Walk on By • and more.
_____02509902 P/V/G..............$19.95

Great Songs of the Sixties, Vol. 2 – Revised Edition

61 more 60s hits: And When I Die • California Dreamin' • Crying • The 59th Street Bridge Song (Feelin' Groovy) • For Once in My Life • Honey • Little Green Apples • MacArthur Park • Me and Bobby McGee • Nowhere Man • Piece of My Heart • Sugar, Sugar • You Made Me So Very Happy • and more.
_____02509904 P/V/G..............$19.95

Great Songs of the Seventies – Revised Edition

This super collection of 70 big hits from the '70s includes: After the Love Has Gone • Afternoon Delight • Annie's Song • Band on the Run • Cold as Ice • FM • Imagine • It's Too Late • Layla • Let It Be • Maggie May • Piano Man • Shelter from the Storm • Superstar • Sweet Baby James • Time in a Bottle • The Way We Were • more!
_____02509917 P/V/G..............$19.95

Prices, contents, and availability subject to change without notice.

Great Songs of the Seventies – Volume 2

Features 58 outstanding '70s songs in rock, pop, country, Broadway and movie genres: American Woman • Baby, I'm-A Want You • Day by Day • Do That to Me One More Time • Dog & Butterfly • Don't Cry Out Loud • Dreamboat Annie • Follow Me • Get Closer • Grease • Heard It in a Love Song • I'll Be There • It's a Heartache • The Loco-Motion • My Eyes Adored You • New Kid in Town • Night Fever • On and On • Sing • Summer Breeze • Tonight's the Night • We Are the Champions • Y.M.C.A. • and more. Includes articles by Cherry Lane Music Company founder Milt Okun, and award-winning music journalist Bruce Pollock.
_____02500322 P/V/G..............$19.95

Great Songs of the Eighties – Revised Edition

This newly revised edition features 50 songs in rock, pop & country styles, plus hits from Broadway and the movies! Songs: Almost Paradise • Angel of the Morning • Do You Really Want to Hurt Me • Endless Love • Flashdance...What a Feeling • Guilty • Hungry Eyes • (Just Like) Starting Over • Let Love Rule • Missing You • Patience • Through the Years • Time After Time • Total Eclipse of the Heart • and more.
_____02502125 P/V/G..............$18.95

Great Songs of the Nineties

This terrific collection features 48 big hits in many styles. Includes: Achy Breaky Heart • Beautiful in My Eyes • Believe • Black Hole Sun • Black Velvet • Blaze of Glory • Building a Mystery • Crash into Me • Fields of Gold • From a Distance • Glycerine • Here and Now • Hold My Hand • I'll Make Love to You • Ironic • Linger • My Heart Will Go On • Waterfalls • Wonderwall • and more.
_____02500040 P/V/G..............$16.95

Great Songs of the Pop Era

Over 50 hits from the pop era, including: Amazed • Annie's Song • Ebony and Ivory • Every Breath You Take • Hey Nineteen • I Want to Know What Love Is • I'm Every Woman • Just the Two of Us • Leaving on a Jet Plane • My Cherie Amour • Raindrops Keep Fallin' on My Head • Rocky Mountain High • This Is the Moment • Time After Time • (I've Had) the Time of My Life • What a Wonderful World • and more!
_____02500043 Easy Piano..............$16.95

CHERRY LANE MUSIC COMPANY
6 East 32nd Street, New York, NY 10016
Quality in Printed Music
Visit Cherry Lane on the Internet at
www.cherrylane.com

Exclusively Distributed By

HAL·LEONARD CORPORATION
7777 W. BLUEMOUND RD. P.O. BOX 13819 MILWAUKEE, WI 53213